Online Safety for Kids

Written by Reema Manchanda

Copyright

Get Cyber Safe: Online Safety for Kids

This revised edition was published in 2026 by Get Cyber Safe Books
First published in 2023

ISBN 978-1-7393348-1-9
www.instagram.com/get.cyber.safe

Dedication

For every curious child taking their first steps online, and for the grown-ups who guide them safely.

Sam sat down next to his mum on the living room sofa. He wanted to download a game on his mum's tablet.

"Mum, why do you always download games for me?" Sam asked, "Can't I do it myself?"

"To download a game, we have to go online," said Mum. "Going online means you're connecting to the internet. The internet is amazing, but it is not always safe for children."

Sam wondered why the internet was not always safe.
People used the internet for lots of reasons.
So, he wanted to know more about it.

"I know!" Mum said, "Why don't we ask Robbie the robot about it?"

Sam thought that was a great idea. Robbie the robot worked with computers every day and was an expert in online safety.

So, Mum took Sam to meet Robbie. Robbie was very happy to see Sam.
"Hi, Sam!" Robbie greeted him, "What can I help you with?"

"I want to know about the internet," Sam said. "Mum says that the internet is not always safe for me.
I want to know why and learn how I can be safe when I'm online."

“I will tell you what I know about online safety,” Robbie said. “When you go online, the internet connects your computer, phone, or tablet to other computers.”

"So many computers are connected together!” said Sam. “If I connect my tablet to the internet, I would be part of this huge group, right?!”

INTERNET

"Correct," said Robbie, "But other computers can get your information. Sometimes, they ask for your information in ways you don't know. It can be a bit like spying."

NAME:
ADDRESS:

"I have seen some messages asking for my name, birthday, and other information…" Sam said, thinking.

"You must not reply to them," Robbie said. "If you feel unsure, ask your mum or dad about it."

NAME:
BIRTHDAY:
EMAIL:

"But how can I make accounts online if I can't give my own name?" asked Sam.

"You don't have to give your real name," explained Robbie.
"You can use a nickname instead. That way, your real name stays private."

Account Name

“Mum usually makes my accounts for me,”
Sam said. “Is that okay?”
“That’s very good!” Robbie smiled. “You’ll be safe when your parents are with you.

Not every website is safe, you see. If you see anything suspicious or confusing, always tell your parents about it.”

“Mum also downloads my games for me,” said Sam.

“That’s great!” Robbie beamed, “Sometimes, you may download harmful software without even knowing. Things like computer viruses can harm your tablet, phone, and computer.”

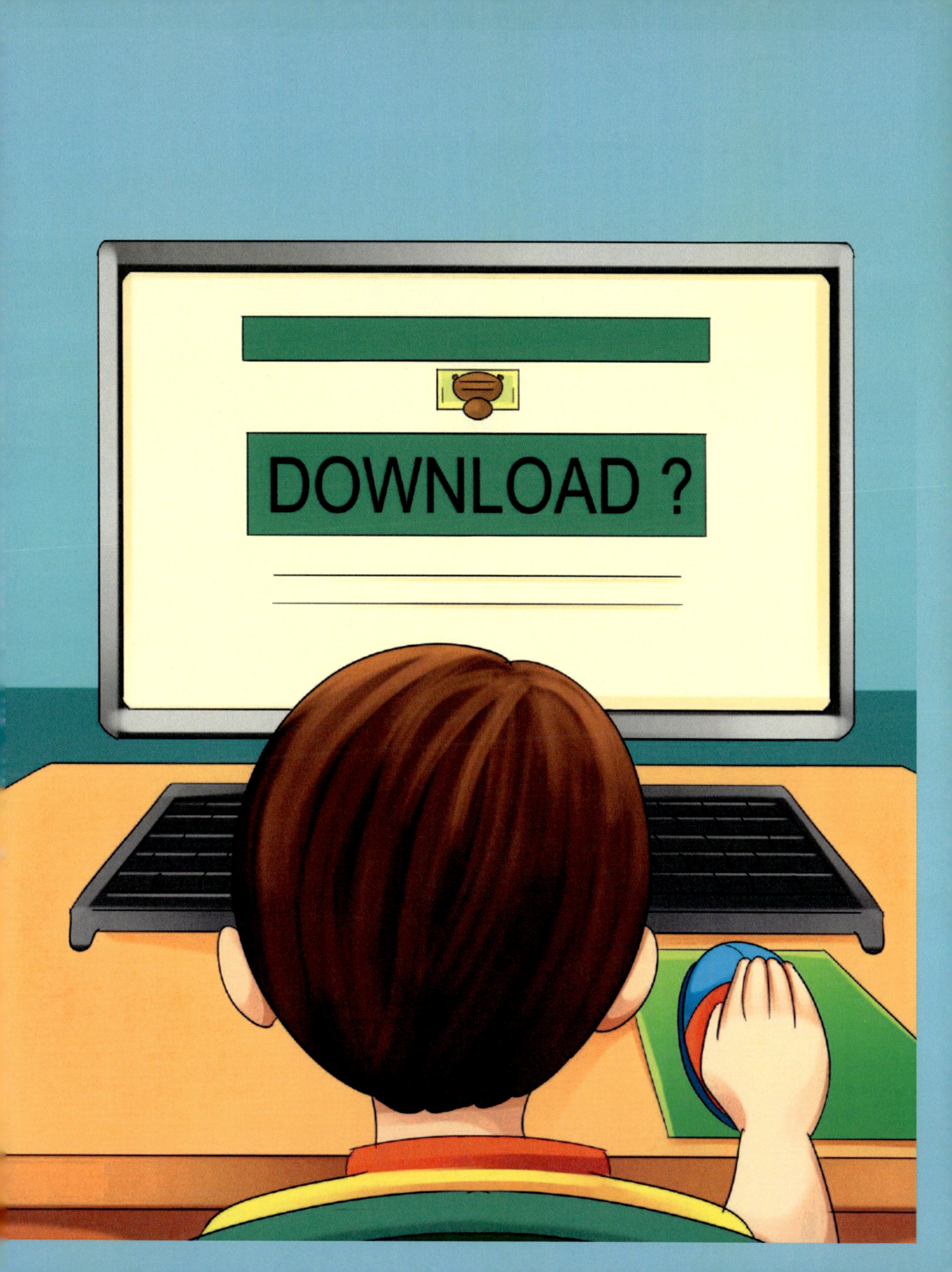
DOWNLOAD ?

"Is it okay to use my picture in accounts?" Sam wanted to know.

"Don't share photos or videos of yourself online," Robbie said seriously, "Always be careful of friends you meet online too."

SHARE
PHOTOS

"Sometimes, I get messages saying that I won a gift," Sam said. "Are those real?"

"Nope!" Robbie shook his head. "Messages and ads like those trick you and collect your information. So, don't ever click on them."

YOU HAVE WON A PRIZE!
$
Accept
Cancel

"Thank you very much for telling me about these things, Robbie," Sam said. "Now I know how important online safety is."

"Always stop and think before you connect!" said Robbie.

Sam and his mum thanked Robbie and left. On the way back home, Mum stopped at the bookstore and bought Sam a book all about online safety. She also promised to download a new game for him!

ONLINE SAFETY

Robbie's Online Safety Rules

1. Ask a grown-up before you go online.
2. Keep your name, address, and birthday private.
3. Use a nickname, not your real name.
4. Never share photos or videos of yourself.
5. Ask a grown-up before downloading anything.
6. Never click on messages that say you have won a prize.
7. If anything online feels strange or confusing, tell a grown-up you trust. Always stop and think before you connect!

A Note for Parents and Teachers

This book is designed to help you introduce online safety to young children in a calm, positive way. The internet is a wonderful part of children's lives, and the habits in this story- keeping personal information private, asking a trusted adult, and pausing before clicking- are the foundations of safe, confident use. After reading, you might like to talk together using these questions:

1. What would you do if a message asked for your name or birthday?
2. Who would you tell if something online made you feel confused or worried?
3. Why do we use nicknames instead of real names online?
4. What did Robbie say we should always do before we connect?

Thank you for reading, and for helping children stop and think before they connect

Made in the USA
Coppell, TX
05 November 2026

11302984R00019